Snapdragons

Stage 7

Gill Howell

Teaching Notes

Cont[ents]

Introducti[on] 2
Vocabular[y] 4
Curriculun[m] 5

Hero

Reading 6
Speaking and listening 8
Writing 8

Toad Swims for his Life!

Reading 9
Speaking and listening 11
Writing 11

The Monster Under the Stairs

Reading 12
Speaking and listening 14
Writing 14

Shy Shark

Reading 15
Speaking and listening 17
Writing 17

I'm Not Wearing That!

Reading 18
Speaking and listening 19
Writing 20

Rory's Lost His Voice

Reading 21
Speaking and listening 23
Writing 23

Oxford Reading Tree resources at this level 24

Introduction

The *Snapdragons* series is a rich mix of different kinds of stories presented as picture books with expertly written text carefully levelled to provide reading practice at each stage in Key Stage 1.

This set of six books at Stage 7 provides further reading practice to encourage children to become confident readers. The stories include elaborated episodes with extended descriptions using more literary language and some challenging vocabulary. They also provide further practice in reading key words, as well as useful vocabulary, such as numbers, colour words and days of the week, relating to the different contexts.

The six books include stories based in familiar settings that reflect everyday life, and the readers will quickly identify with the family members, school friends and pets and recognise their experiences. There are also stories about fantasy worlds including animal fantasy tales, and a story in a historic setting as well as some jokes and puzzles.

Children are encouraged to look at the illustrations for visual cues to the words in the text, and to find out what is happening in the story. The picture book presentation will also encourage children to tell the story in their own words so that they develop their oral skills.

How to introduce the books

Before reading the story for guided or independent reading, always read the title and talk about the picture on the cover.

Go through the book together, looking at the pictures and talking about them. If there are context words (listed in the chart on page 4) that are new or unfamiliar, point them out and read them with the children. Read the story to the children, encouraging confident children to join in with you.

This booklet provides prompts and suggestions for using the books in groups and for guided, group and independent activities, matched to text, sentence and word level objectives. There are also separate Guided Reading Cards available for six titles at each stage. Suggestions are also provided for speaking and listening activities, writing activities, and cross-curricular links. You can use these suggestions to follow on from your reading or at another time.

Reading notes are also provided in each book. They can be found on the inside front and back covers of each book. These suggest friendly prompts and activities for parents or carers reading with their children at home.

Reading skills

Stage 7 develops:
- strategies for independent reading, including consolidation of irregular phonological and spelling patterns
- insights into feelings and motivation of characters
- a wider sight vocabulary
- awareness of other viewpoints
- confidence through familiarity with the characters and the format
- sustained independent writing.

Vocabulary chart

Stage 7		
Hero	Year 2 High frequency words	about after an back be bed but call came could did do don't from good got had has have her him his home house jump(ed) just little made more new next night not now old one out over put ran should so that their them then there us very water were what will with would
	Context words	puppy hero newspapers basket bowl brush howl puddle breakfast clock teddy bottle blanket
Toad Swims for his Life!	Year 2 High frequency words	about after as back but can't could did do don't down from had have his home last laugh little make much name not now put saw so that them then there these three two very want water way were when who will with your
	Context words	Toad pool Shark champion Snake Tiger Crocodile crowd jelly circle
The Monster Under the Stairs	Year 2 High frequency words	after again as back be but by called came could did do don't door from got had have help(ed) her him his if jump(ed) just laugh little live made night not now off old one or out over pull(ed) put ran sister so some that their them then there too is very want way were what who will with
	Context words	Imran Shaz truck Fang monster cupboard kitchen coat shoes teddy bedroom wardrobe
Shy Shark	Year 2 High frequency words	about again as be because but called came can't could down first from got had has him how if jump(ed) little many most one out over pull(ed) push(ed) saw so some that their them then there three us very want water were when will with would
	Context words	Shy Shark jellyfish starfish clown fish creatures dolphins seahorse trapped
I'm Not Wearing That!	Year 2 High frequency words	again but came did don't from girl got have her here him his home little make more name new night not now off old one our out put so that them then too took want when will with 7 days of the week colour words: red yellow blue white green purple pink orange
	Context words	Yorik Olaf Erika Viking bluebirds whales trousers sunset buttercups gold cloak volcanoes shield necklace helmet tongue rainbow
Rory's Lost His Voice	Year 2 High frequency words	about again back be because bed boy but by call came can't did do don't door down from have here him his if last little love more much must next night not off one out over pull(ed) school so that their then there three too very what when where will with your
	Context words	Rory football voice hurt doctor Mohammed window final throat medicine television goal

Curriculum coverage chart

Stage 7	Speaking and listening	Reading	Writing
Hero			
NLS/SLL	T7/Y2T2 17	T6, S2, W4	T14
Scotland	Level A/B	Level A/B	Level A/B
N. Ireland	Activities: a, b, c Outcomes: b, c, d	Activities: a, b, c Outcomes: b, c, d, e, f, k	Outcomes: a, b, c, f, h
Wales	Range: 1, 5 Skills: 1, 2, 4	Range: 1, 2, 4, 5, 6 Skills: 1, 2	Range: 1, 2, 3, 4, 7 Skills: 1, 2, 3, 5, 6, 7, 8
Toad Swims for his Life!			
NLS/SLL	Y2T2 17	T3, T6, S2, W5	T13
Scotland	Level A/B	Level A/B	Level A/B
N. Ireland	Activities: a, b, f, g Outcomes: a, b, c, e	Activities: a, b, c Outcomes: b, c, d, e, f, k	Outcomes: a, b, c, h, i
Wales	Range: 1 Skills: 1, 2, 3, 4	Range: 1, 2, 4, 5, 6 Skills: 1, 2	Range: 1, 2, 3, 7 Skills: 1, 3, 4, 7, 8
The Monster under the Stairs			
NLS/SLL	Y2T2 20	T7, S2, W1	T14
Scotland	Level A/B	Level A/B	Level A/B
N. Ireland	Activities: a, b, c Outcomes: a, b, c, d	Activities: a, b, c, e Outcomes: b, c, d, e, f, k	Outcomes: a, b, c, h, i
Wales	Range: 1, 5, 6 Skills: 1, 2, 3, 4	Range: 1, 2, 4, 5, 6 Skills: 1, 2	Range: 1, 2, 3, 7 Skills: 1, 2, 3, 7, 8
Shy Shark			
NLS/SLL	T7/Y2T2 17, 19	T5, S2, W3	T14
Scotland	Level A/B	Level A/B	Level A/B
N. Ireland	Activities: a, b, c Outcomes: b, d	Activities: a, b, e Outcomes: b, c, d, e, f, k	Outcomes: a, b, c, f, h, i
Wales	Range: 1, 2, 5 Skills: 1, 2, 3, 4	Range: 1, 2, 4, 5, 6 Skills: 1, 2	Range: 1, 2, 3, 4, 7 Skills: 1, 2, 3, 5, 7, 8
I'm Not Wearing That!			
NLS/SLL	T7	T7, S8, W2	T15
Scotland	Level A/B	Level A/B	Level A/B
N. Ireland	Activities: a, b, c Outcomes: a, b, c, d	Activities: a, b, c, e Outcomes: b, c, d, e, f, k	Outcomes: a, b, c, h, i
Wales	Range: 1, 5 Skills: 2, 3	Range: 1, 2, 4, 5, 6 Skills: 1, 2	Range: 1, 2, 3, 4, 7 Skills: 1, 3, 5, 7, 8
Rory's Lost His Voice			
NLS/SLL	S5/Y2T2 17	T6, S5, W5	T14
Scotland	Level A/B	Level A/B	Level A/B
N. Ireland	Activities: a, e, f, g Outcomes: a, b, c	Activities: a, b, e Outcomes: b, c, d, e, f, k	Outcomes: a, b, c, h, i
Wales	Range: 1 Skills: 1, 2, 3	Range: 1, 2, 4, 5, 6 Skills: 1, 2	Range: 1, 2, 3, 6, 7 Skills: 1, 3, 5, 7, 8

Hero

Reading the story

Introducing the story

- Look together at the front cover, read the title and the author's name.
- Discuss the title, and then ask the children what a hero is or does.
- Ask them if anyone on the cover looks like a hero.
- Ask the children to look briefly through the book to establish the setting.

During reading

- Ask the children to read in a quiet voice as you listen to them individually.
- Praise the children when they read with confidence and self-correct without prompting.
- Prompt the children to use different strategies to work out new words and make sense of their reading.
- Encourage the children to read the dialogue in an expressive tone, making use of punctuation to help them.

Observing Check that the children:
- are confident about identifying dialogue denoted by speech marks.

Group and independent reading activities

Text level work

Range familiar setting/predictable and patterned language

Objective To identify and describe characters, expressing own views and using words and phrases from texts (T6).

- Ask the children to write the names of the four characters in the story (Dad, Ben, Amy and Hero).
- Ask the children to take one character at a time and search through the text to identify any words or phrases that give clues to their character and personality, e.g. p2 "Dad smiled"; p4 "Dad gently picked"; p9 "Dad got cross".

Observing ● Ask the children to add other words from their own knowledge to describe each character, by thinking about what they do and say to each other, and using the illustrations.

Observing Do the children read between the lines (use inference) to think about the characters?

Sentence level work

Objective To read aloud with intonation and expression appropriate to the grammar and punctuation (sentences, speech marks, exclamation marks) (S2).

- Ask the children to work in groups of three, and to read only the spoken words aloud, each taking the role of Dad, Ben or Amy.
- Ask them to read the words in the way they think each character would say them, by noting the punctuation (question marks and exclamation marks) and any verbs that describe speech, e.g. whispered, shouted.
- Ask them to think about their personalities (see Text level activity).

Observing Do the children accurately identify speech punctuation?

Word level work

Objective To split familiar oral and written compound words into their component parts (W4).

- Ask the children: *What did Dad use to protect the floor from Hero's puddles?* and write "newspaper" on the board.
- Ask the children to identify two separate smaller words in this word.
- Ask them to search through the text and find any other words that are made by combining two smaller words. ("downstairs", "breakfast", "lunchtime", "bathroom", "cupboard", "cardboard", "upstairs", "everyone")
- If necessary, explain the meaning and origin of "breakfast" and "cupboard".
- Write the words the children have found on the board, and ask them to suggest other compound words they know of. Add them to the list.
- The children could add any new words from the list to their word banks.

Observing Do the children scan the text for longer words to identify compound words?

Speaking and listening activities

Objectives To prepare and re-tell stories individually and through role-play in groups, using dialogue and narrative from the text (T7); To tell real and imagined stories using the conventions of familiar story language (Y2T2 17).

- Ask the children to work in groups of four, and take the characters of Dad, Ben, Amy and Hero.
- Ask the children to discuss in groups how to turn the story into a short play, and to rehearse it.
- Ask some of the groups to perform their play for the rest of the class.

Cross-curricular link
◀▶ PSHE: people and other living things have needs, and they have responsibilities to meet them

Writing

Objective To write character profiles, e.g. simple descriptions, posters, passports, using key words and phrases that describe or are spoken by characters in the text (T14).

- Ask the children to imagine the farmer wrote an advertisement about Hero.
- Together, draw up a list of words and phrases that describe the puppy.
- Ask the children to draw a picture to illustrate their advertisement, and to choose words and phrases that would make people want the puppy.
- Make a class display of the advertisements.

Toad Swims for his Life!

Reading the story

Introducing the story

- Look together at the front cover, read the title and the author's name.
- Ask the children to find Toad in the illustration, and the word in the title. Discuss the phrase "for his life" with the children. Ask them what they think Toad could be frightened of.
- Ask the children to look briefly through the book to establish the setting and confirm their ideas.
- Look at the speech and thought bubbles on pages 3, 4 and 5. Ask the children what is different about each. Establish which is a thought bubble, and which is a speech bubble, and the purpose of the speech bubbles with zigzag lines.

During reading

- Ask the children to read in a quiet voice as you listen to them individually.
- Praise the children when they read with confidence and self-correct without prompting.
- On page 5, ask the children to read the speech bubble, emphasising the alliteration.
- Prompt the children to think carefully about reading the lines of text, the speech bubbles and the thought bubbles in the right order to make sense of what is happening.
- On page 18, check that the children read the text in the right order.
- Encourage the children to read the speech bubbles in an expressive tone, to differentiate between the animals.

Observing Check that the children:
- use an appropriate strategy to work out new or difficult words.

Group and independent reading activities

Text level work

Range fantasy world/predictable and patterned language

Objectives To discuss and compare story themes (T3); To identify and describe characters, expressing own views and using words and phrases from texts (T6).

- Ask the children to briefly retell the story in their own words. Ask them to suggest some words to describe Toad's character, and find evidence in the text.
- If necessary, point out that Toad plays a trick on the other characters, so he might be described as clever.
- Ask the children to think of other stories they have read where one animal tricks the others in the story, e.g. "Little Mouse Deer", "The Tortoise and the Hare", "Anansi Stories".
- Ask the children to think of a sentence to describe the story theme.

Observing Do the children recognise the theme of cleverness being more important than just strength and aggression?

Sentence level work

Objective To read aloud with intonation and expression appropriate to the grammar and punctuation (sentences, speech marks, exclamation marks) (S2).

- Ask the children to work in groups of six, and to read only the speech bubbles aloud, each taking the role of one of the characters.
- Ask them to read the crowd's words together.
- Ask the children to read the words as they think each character would say them, using expressive voices.

Observing Do the children read the speech bubbles, and leave out Toad's thought bubbles?

Word level work

Objective To discriminate, orally, syllables in multi-syllabic words using children's names and words from their reading. Extend to written forms and note syllable boundary in speech and writing (W5).

- Ask the children to read "Welcome to the Animal Games" on page 2, and to count the syllables in each word.
- Ask them to write "Animal" on their boards, and to search through the text and find any other 3-syllable words and add them to the list. ("champion", "overtake", "crocodile", "anything", "suddenly", "forgotten", "terrible")

- Encourage the children to check the number of syllables by speaking them carefully aloud.
- The children could add any new words from the list to their word banks.

Observing Do the children understand that long words do not necessarily have more syllables (e.g. "shivered" and "metres" both are 2-syllable words although one word has more letters than the other)?

Speaking and listening activities

Objective To tell real and imagined stories using the conventions of familiar story language (Y2T2 17).

- Ask the children if any of them have been in a race.
- Encourage the children to describe what happened to the rest of the group.
- Ask some of the children to imagine what would happen if they were in a race against the characters from the story, and describe it for the rest of the group.

Cross-curricular link
◀▶ PSHE: to take part in discussions with one person and the whole class

Writing

Objective To use story settings from reading, e.g. re-describe, use in own writing, write a different story in the same setting (T13).

- Discuss the swimming pool setting in the story with the children.
- Draw up a list of words that describe it using the children's suggestions.
- Prompt the children to think about what they would see, hear and feel in this setting.
- Ask the children to write a paragraph in their own words to describe the setting.

The Monster Under the Stairs

Reading the story

Introducing the story

- Look together at the front cover, read the title and the author's name.
- Ask: *What do you think the two children are doing?*
- Look through the book and identify any new or unfamiliar vocabulary, e.g. p7 "believe", "frightened".
- Look briefly through the book at the illustrations to establish the setting.

During reading

- Ask the children to read in a quiet voice as you listen to them individually.
- Ask the children to point out the speech marks in dialogue where the reporting clause comes in the middle of the spoken words, and ask them to say who is speaking the words.
- Encourage the children to read the dialogue between Imran and Shaz in an expressive tone.
- Praise the children when they read with confidence and self-correct without prompting.
- On page 10, ask: *Why is the word "was" written in italics? How does it affect the way you read it?*
- Encourage the children to read "WHOO-OO-OO-HOOO!" expressively.

Observing Check that the children:
- use their knowledge of sounds and familiar letter strings to work out unfamiliar words.

Group and independent reading activities

Text level work

Range familiar setting/predictable and patterned language

Objective To prepare and re-tell stories individually and through role-play in groups, using dialogue and narrative from the text (T7).

- Ask the children to take turns to sit in the hot seat, and take the role of Imran or Shaz.
- Ask them to retell the events of the story using "I", first person verbs.
- Ask the rest of the children to ask them questions about their feelings.

Observing Are the children able to put themselves into role, and to think about reasons for actions?

Sentence level work

Objective To read aloud with intonation and expression appropriate to the grammar and punctuation (S2).

- Ask the children to work with a partner. Ask them to read the spoken words of Imran and Shaz, each taking one role.
- Remind the children to observe where the speech marks denote the start and end of speech.

Observing Do the children read with expressive voices, noticing question marks and exclamation marks?

Word level work

Objective To secure the reading and spelling of words containing different spellings of the long vowel phonemes from Year 1 (W1).

- Ask the children to find the word "leave" on page 4. Ask them to say the vowel sound aloud, and to write it on their boards ("ea").
- Ask them to search through the text and find other words with the same long "ee" sound, and to write them on their boards in groups according to their spelling patterns. ("teeth", "eat", "believe", "see", "he", "she", "beating", "feeling", "screamed", "clear", "peered", "keep", "clean")
- Ask the children to practise spelling the words by using Read, Cover, Write and Check.
- The children could add any new words from the list to their word banks.

Observing Do the children note that the most common spelling pattern is either "ee" or "ea"?

Speaking and listening activities

Objective To consider how mood and atmosphere are created in a live or recorded performance (Y2T2 20).

- Discuss the story with the children, looking at the last sentences on pages 9, 13 and 17. Ask: *Does this make you feel unsure about what will happen? Do you want to turn the page to find out?*
- Ask the children to think about how the author created suspense in the story.
- Ask them to work with a partner and act out Imran and Shaz's parts, thinking about how to create a scary mood for the audience.
- Ask some of the children to perform for the rest of the class.

Cross-curricular link
◀▶ PSHE: to take part in discussions with one person and the whole class

Writing

Objective To write character profiles, e.g. simple descriptions (T14).

- Ask the children to read Imran's description of Fang on page 6.
- Ask them to work with a partner and each write a simple description of their own "Monster Under the Stairs".
- Tell the children to swap descriptions and each draw the other's monster based on their partner's description.

Shy Shark

Reading the story

Introducing the story

- Look together at the front cover, read the title and the author's name.
- Ask: *What do we usually think about sharks? What do you think is different about this one?*
- Look through the book, focusing on the illustrations to confirm the children's ideas.
- Look at the text on pages 2 and 3. Explain that the 3 dots (ellipsis) are used to show a pause that anticipates something to come. Read the text aloud as a model for the children.
- Identify any new or unfamiliar vocabulary, e.g. p5 "fierce", p6 "creatures".

During reading

- Ask the children to read in a quiet voice as you listen to them individually.
- On page 2, ask *Which words rhyme here?* ("tiny shiny")
- On page 4, encourage the children to read "SHARKS!" expressively.
- Encourage the children to pause at the end of page 5 before turning over.
- Praise the children when they read with confidence and self-correct without prompting.
- On page 8, ask the children to point out the alliteration ("Shy Shark", "dash and dart", "joke with the jelly fish").
- On page 14, praise children who read with expression, pausing at the punctuation.
- On pages 23 and 24, ask the children why they think the author chose to begin two sentences with "And". Ask them how the text would change if "And" was omitted. Encourage the children to think about how an author brings emphasis to parts of the story.

Observing Check that the children:
- read with pace and fluency, self-correcting where necessary.

Group and independent reading activities

Text level work

Range fantasy world/predictable and patterned language

Objective To discuss story settings: to compare differences; to locate key words and phrases in text; to consider how different settings influence events and behaviour (T5).

- Ask the children to say where the story is set. Encourage the children to look through the book at the illustrations and suggest words that describe the setting.
- Ask the children to suggest a sound that is like the sea. Prompt them, if necessary, to say "sshh", or "sss".
- Ask the children to look through the text and find examples of pages where the author has used lots of words with these sounds in them.

Observing Do the children read words aloud to identify the sounds?

Sentence level work

Objective To read aloud with intonation and expression appropriate to the grammar and punctuation (S2).

- Ask the children to work with a partner.
- Ask them to take turns to read alternate pages aloud to each other.
- Remind them to use expressive voices.

Observing Do the children take note of the punctuation?

Word level work

Objective To read and spell words containing the digraph *'wh'*, *'ph'*, *'ch'* (W3).

- Ask the children to be word detectives.
- Write the digraph "wh" on the board. Ask the children to say the sound aloud.
- Ask them to look through the text and find any words with this sound and spelling. ("why", "what", "Whoosh")
- Write the digraph "ph" on the board. Ask the children to say the sound aloud.
- Ask the children to find the word with this sound and spelling in the text. ("dolphin")

Shy Shark

- Encourage the children to practise spelling the words by using Read, Cover, Write and Check.
- Ask the children to add the words to their personal word banks.

Observing Do the children differentiate between words with the letter "f" and the "ph" digraph?

Speaking and listening activities

Objectives To prepare and re-tell stories individually and through role-play in groups, using dialogue and narrative from text (T7); To tell real and imagined stories using the conventions of familiar story language (Y2T2 17); To ensure everyone contributes, allocate tasks, consider alternatives and reach agreement (Y2T2 19).

- Provide the children with stick puppets of all the sea creatures in the story (see Cross-curricular activity below).
- Ask the children in groups to act out the story.
- Encourage them to add dialogue, so that everyone is included, e.g. words to describe how they swim or behave in the sea, what they say when they see a shark.
- Groups can be any size, as the number of performers can be large enough for shoals of fish.
- Encourage the children to use the stick puppets to imitate the movement of the different sea creatures, e.g. sea horses, sea snakes, starfish.
- Ask some of the children to perform for the rest of the class.

Cross-curricular link
◀▶ Art: painting fish/sea creature stick puppets or masks

Writing

Objective To write character profiles, e.g. simple descriptions (T14).

- Ask the children to imagine that Shy Shark wants to advertise for a friend.
- Discuss the wording that Shy Shark might use to encourage someone to be his friend. Model writing it for the children, e.g. "Shy friendly shark wants a friend to swim with."
- Ask the children to draw a poster of Shy Shark, and add descriptions of his personality. Display their posters on the wall.

I'm Not Wearing That!

Reading the story

Introducing the story

- Look together at the front cover, read the title and the author's name.
- Ask the children to suggest where they think the story is set.
- Read page 2 together, identifying the names Yorik, Olaf and Erika in print and matching them with the illustrations. Ask the children to suggest what the story will be about.
- Look through the book, focusing on the illustrations to confirm the children's ideas.

During reading

- Ask the children to read in a quiet voice as you listen to them individually.
- On page 10, if children have difficulty with "shield" or "mouldy", ask them to check the illustration, and predict a word that makes sense. If they still struggle, tell them the word so they don't lose the sense of the story.
- Praise the children when they read with confidence and self-correct without prompting.
- Encourage the children to read with expression, taking notice of the grammar and punctuation.
- Ask: *How does Mr Viking persuade Erika to wear different colours?*

Observing Check that the children:
- read the dialogue in an expressive tone.

Group and independent reading activities

Text level work

Range predictable and patterned language/from another culture

Objective To prepare and re-tell stories individually and through role-play in groups, using dialogue and narrative from text (T7).

- Ask the children to work with a partner, and act out the story together by reading Dad and Erika's spoken words from the story.

- Ask some of the children to perform for the others.
- Discuss whether the story still makes sense.
- Ask how adding a narrator would improve their retellings.

Observing Do the children read the dialogue expressively?

Sentence level work

Objective To use commas to separate items in a list (S8).

- Ask the children to read through the text and identify the items of clothing and the colour words used.
- Write the beginning of a sentence on the board, e.g. "In the story, Erika wears…".
- Ask the children to complete the sentence with a list of the coloured clothes from the story.

Observing Do the children use commas to separate the items?

Word level work

Objective The common spelling patterns for the vowel phonemes: 'air', 'or', 'er' (Appendix list 3) (W2).

- Ask the children to be word detectives.
- Write the word "wear" on the board.
- Ask them to look through the text and find any words with this sound. ("wear", "spare", "pair")
- Ask the children to write each word as a heading, and to add other words from their knowledge grouped by spelling pattern.

Observing Do the children recognise how the words "wear" and "dear" on page 3 have the same spelling pattern but different sounds?

Speaking and listening activities

Objective To prepare and re-tell stories individually and through role-play in groups, using dialogue and narrative from text (T7).

- Ask the children about the clothes they prefer to wear. Do they have a favourite colour?
- Ask them if they think they are like Erika in the story.

I'm Not Wearing That!

- Choose some children to take turns to sit in the hot seat as Erika, and describe what happened when Mrs Viking left her in Mr Viking's care.

Cross-curricular link
◀▶ Art and Design: self portrait

Writing

Objective To use structures from poems as a basis for writing, by extending or substituting elements, inventing own lines, verses; to make class collections, illustrate with captions; to write own poems from initial jottings and words (T15).

- Ask the children to turn to pages 4–5 and read the two ways "blue" is described. Write them on the board:
    Blue is the colour of little bluebirds.
    Blue is the colour of giant blue whales.
- Ask the children to search through the rest of the text and find two ways of describing each colour.
- Encourage the children to use the sentences on the board as a model for writing the colour descriptions as a poem.
- Suggest they add other colours and descriptions, using a contrasting "weak" image, followed by a "powerful" image.

Rory's Lost His Voice

Reading the story

Introducing the story

- Look together at the front cover, read the title and the author's name.
- Discuss the title, and ask the children what is happening in the illustration.
- Ask them to suggest what they think the story will be about.
- Ask the children to look briefly through the book to establish the setting.

During reading

- Ask the children to read in a quiet voice as you listen to them individually.
- Praise the children when they read with confidence and self-correct without prompting.
- Prompt the children to use different strategies to work out new words and make sense of their reading.
- Encourage the children to read the dialogue in an expressive tone, raising their voice at question marks, and reading words in bold with emphasis.
- Ask the children to read the last line on page 11. Ask them why they think the author wrote this line as three sentences instead of one. Ask: *How does it affect your reading?* Praise when children use full stops to pause.

Observing Check that the children:
- read familiar words with pace and confidence.

Group and independent reading activities

Text level work

Range familiar setting/predictable and patterned language

Objective To identify and describe characters, expressing own views and using words and phrases from texts (T6).

- Ask the children to suggest who the main characters are in the story.

- Write their suggestions on the board and discuss what each character is like, e.g. Rory: a chatterbox; Mohammed: a joker.
- Ask them to write down the names of the main characters, and to look through the text and find words or phrases to support their ideas about each character.
- Ask the children to read out their findings, and discuss how the author portrays each character, e.g. making a direct statement (page 2), or through describing their actions, or dialogue.

Observing Are the children able to 'read between the lines' to draw their own conclusions?

Sentence level work

Objective To use verb tenses with increasing accuracy in speaking and writing, e.g. *catch/caught, see/saw, go/went* and to use past tense consistently for narration (S5).

- Look together at pages 2 and 3. Ask the children to find the past tense verbs on these pages. ("stopped", "did", "talked", "woke", "hurt", "breathed", "swallowed")
- Write the list of verbs in two columns: regular "–ed" endings and irregular verbs.
- Ask the children to change the irregular verbs from past to present tense.
- Ask the children to search the text up to pages 10 and 11, and find other irregular past tense verbs, and change them to the present tense. ("was"/"is", "said"/"say", "came"/"come", "went"/"go")

Observing Do the children scan the lines of text, or do they need to read each word to find the verbs?

Word level work

Objective To discriminate, orally, syllables in multi-syllabic words using children's names and words from their reading. Extend to written forms and note syllable boundary in speech and writing (W5).

- Ask the children to work with a partner. Encourage the children to look through the text and write down words with three or more syllables.
- Ask them to read the words to their partners and discuss together where the syllables start and end.

- Ask the children to write the words with a line between each syllable and read them aloud again, e.g. com/pu/ter, an/y/where, med/i/cine, tel/e/vis/ion.
- Ask them to practise spelling the words using Look, Cover, Write and Check.
- The children could add any new words from the list to their word banks.

Observing Do the children use the syllable boundaries to help them spell?

Speaking and listening activities

Objectives To use verb tenses with increasing accuracy in speaking and writing, and to use past tense consistently for narration (S5); To tell real and imagined stories using the conventions of familiar story language (Y2T2 17).

- Ask the children to describe an occasion when they have been ill and stayed in bed.
- Encourage them to use past tense consistently, and to use connectives to link their recounts, e.g. after a while, later, at last.

Cross-curricular link
◀▶ PSHE: people and other living things have needs, and they have responsibilities to meet them

Writing

Objective To write character profiles, e.g. simple descriptions, posters, passports, using key words and phrases that describe or are spoken by characters in the text (T14).

- Ask the children to choose one character from the story. Tell them to look through the text and illustrations and write a short description of the character.
- Ask the children to read their description to a partner, without using the character's name. Can their partner say who is being described?

Oxford Reading Tree resources at this level

There is a range of material available at a similar level to these stories which can be used for consolidation or extension.

Stage 7

Teacher support
- Teacher's Handbook
- Take-Home Card for each story
- Storytapes
- Woodpeckers Photocopy Masters
- Group Activity Sheets Book 3 Stages 6–9
- ORT Games Stages 6–9

Further reading
- Oxford Reading Tree Storybooks for Core Reading
- Woodpeckers Phonics Anthologies 2–5
- Playscripts Stages 6 & 7
- Fireflies Non-Fiction
- Fact Finders Units D and E
- Glow-worms Poetry

Electronic
- Clip Art
- Stage 6 & 7 Talking Stories
- ORT Online www.OxfordReadingTree.com
- Floppy and Friends

OXFORD
UNIVERSITY PRESS

Great Clarendon Street, Oxford OX2 6DP

Oxford University Press is a department of the University of Oxford. It furthers the University's objective of excellence in research, scholarship, and education by publishing worldwide in

Oxford New York

Auckland Cape Town Dar es Salaam Hong Kong Karachi Kuala Lumpur Madrid Melbourne Mexico City Nairobi New Delhi Shanghai Taipei Toronto

With offices in

Argentina Austria Brazil Chile Czech Republic France Greece Guatemala Hungary Italy Japan Poland Portugal Singapore South Korea Switzerland Thailand Turkey Ukraine Vietnam

Oxford is a registered trade mark of Oxford University Press in the UK and in certain other countries

© Oxford University Press 2005

The moral rights of the author have been asserted

Database right Oxford University Press (maker)

First published 2005

All rights reserved. No part of this publication may be reproduced, stored in a retrieval system, or transmitted, in any form or by any means, without the prior permission in writing of Oxford University Press, or as expressly permitted by law, or under terms agreed with the appropriate reprographics rights organization. Enquiries concerning reproduction outside the scope of the above should be sent to the Rights Department, Oxford University Press, at the address above

You must not circulate this book in any other binding or cover and you must impose this same condition on any acquirer

British Library Cataloguing in Publication Data

Data available

Series adviser Shirley Bickler

Cover illustration David Mostyn

Teacher's Notes: ISBN 978-0-19-845558-5

20 19 18 17

Page make-up by Fakenham Photosetting, Fakenham, Norfolk

Printed in China by Imago